What are dinosaurs?

Bobbie Kalman

🌳 Crabtree Publishing Company

www.crabtreebooks.com

Created by Bobbie Kalman

Author and Editor-in-Chief
Bobbie Kalman

Reading consultant
Elaine Hurst

Editors
Kathy Middleton
Crystal Sikkens

Design
Bobbie Kalman
Katherine Berti

Photo research
Bobbie Kalman

**Production coordinator
and Prepress technician**
Katherine Berti

Illustrations
Katherine Berti: page 21 (top right)
Bonna Rouse: pages 6, 11 (bottom),
    23 (crests)

Photographs
BigStockPhoto: pages 6, 23 (herbivores)
Other photographs by Shutterstock

Library and Archives Canada Cataloguing in Publication

Kalman, Bobbie, 1947-
    What are dinosaurs? / Bobbie Kalman.

(My world)
Includes index.
ISBN 978-0-7787-9514-8 (bound).--ISBN 978-0-7787-9539-1 (pbk.)

    1. Dinosaurs--Juvenile literature. I. Title. II. Series: My world
(St. Catharines, Ont.)

QE861.5.K34 2011   j567.9   C2010-901977-6

Library of Congress Cataloging-in-Publication Data

Kalman, Bobbie.
    What are dinosaurs? / Bobbie Kalman.
        p. cm. -- (My world)
    Includes index.
    ISBN 978-0-7787-9539-1 (pbk. : alk. paper) -- ISBN 978-0-7787-9514-8
(reinforced lib. bdg. : alk. paper)
    1. Dinosaurs--Juvenile literature. I. Title.

QE861.5.K32 2011
567.9--dc22

                                                                    2010011304

Crabtree Publishing Company

www.crabtreebooks.com   1-800-387-7650

Printed in China/072010/AP20100226

Published in Canada
Crabtree Publishing
616 Welland Ave.
St. Catharines, Ontario
L2M 5V6

Published in the United States
Crabtree Publishing
PMB 59051
350 Fifth Avenue, 59th Floor
New York, New York 10118

Published in the United Kingdom
Crabtree Publishing
Maritime House
Basin Road North, Hove
BN41 1WR

Published in Australia
Crabtree Publishing
386 Mt. Alexander Rd.
Ascot Vale (Melbourne)
VIC 3032

What is in this book?

What are dinosaurs?

Dinosaurs lived long ago.

There are no dinosaurs alive today.

Dinosaurs were **reptiles**.

Reptiles are animals with **backbones**.

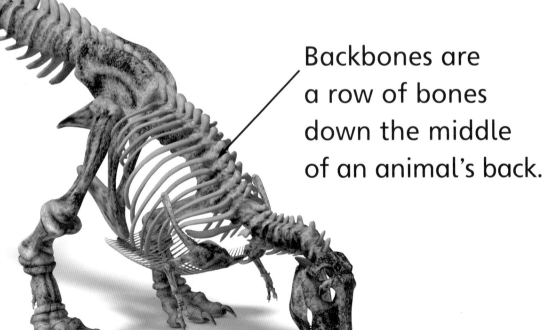

Backbones are
a row of bones
down the middle
of an animal's back.

4

Reptiles have **scales**.
Scales are patches
of hard, dry skin.
Scales protected
a dinosaur's
body.

scales

5

Hatching from eggs

Dinosaur babies **hatched** from eggs.
To hatch is to break out of an egg.

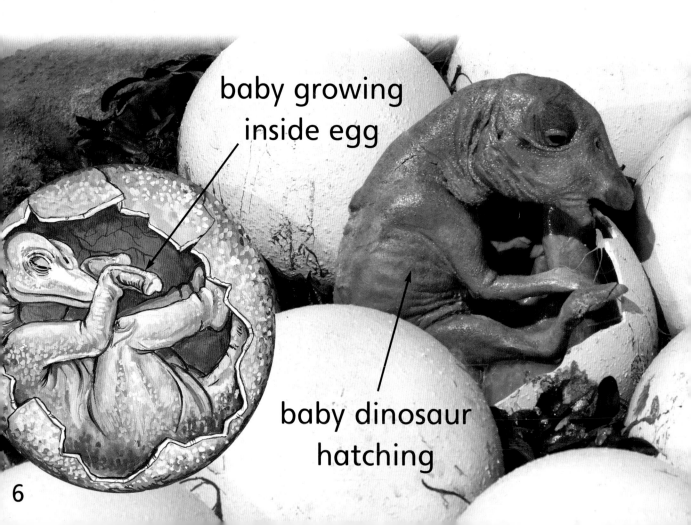

baby growing
inside egg

baby dinosaur
hatching

Some baby dinosaurs stayed close
to their mothers.
The mothers helped them find food to eat.

Two or four legs?

Some dinosaurs walked on two legs.

Their back legs were long and strong.

Their front legs were more like arms.

Some dinosaurs walked on all four legs. Their strong front legs helped support their heavy bodies.

Plant eaters

Some dinosaurs were **herbivores**.

Herbivores are animals that eat plants.

Some plant-eating dinosaurs were huge!

Some of the longest, tallest, and heaviest dinosaurs were herbivores.

Hadrosaurus

Some herbivores
had colorful heads.
Some had **crests**.

crest

11

Meat-eating dinosaurs

Carnivores are meat-eating animals.
Dinosaur carnivores had big, sharp teeth.

Tyrannosaurus Rex

Can you say the name of this dinosaur?

Aucasaurus

This carnivore was medium-sized.

It had very small hands.

Sharp dinosaurs

Some dinosaurs
were covered with
bony **plates**.
The plates
protected them
from enemies.

plate

Stegosaurus

This dinosaur had
bony plates on its body.
It used its spiky tail like a club
to fight its enemies.

club

sharp plates
(spines)

Talarurus

This dinosaur had
very sharp plates.
It also had a big club
at the end of its tail.

15

Horns on their heads

Some dinosaurs had **horns** on their heads and **frills** that protected their necks. Their mouths were like **beaks**. These dinosaurs ate plants.

Triceratops

frill

horns

This dinosaur had three horns.

beak

This dinosaur
had two horns.

This dinosaur
had one horn
and four to six
frill spines.

Styracosaurus

Diceratops

Einiosaurus

This dinosaur had a
curved horn and
two large horns
on its neck frill.

17

The biggest carnivore

This dinosaur was the biggest meat-eating dinosaur. Its **skull** was long and narrow.

skull

Spinosaurus

18

Along its back was a large **sail** that ran from its neck down to its tail.

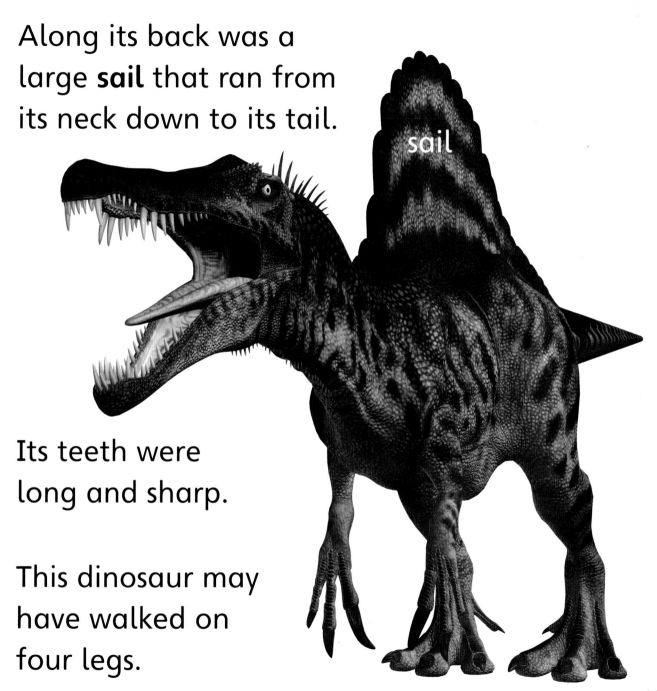

sail

Its teeth were long and sharp.

This dinosaur may have walked on four legs.

Was it a dinosaur?

Other reptiles
lived during
the same time
that dinosaurs lived.
Some had wings
and could fly,
but they were
not dinosaurs.
Dinosaurs did not fly.

Pterosaur

Some reptiles lived in oceans during the time of the dinosaurs, but they were not dinosaurs. Dinosaurs did not live in oceans.

Ichthyosaurus

Mosasaurus

Plesiosaurus

Match them up!

Each of the animals with a number
is like one of the dinosaurs with a letter.
How is each pair alike?

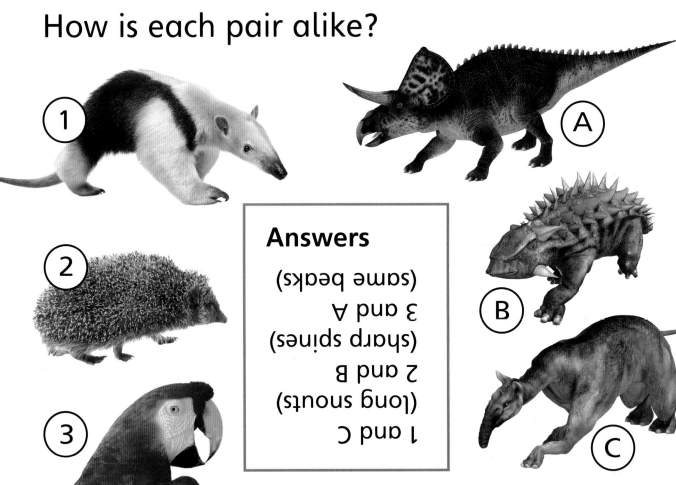

Answers

(same beaks)
3 and A
(sharp spines)
2 and B
(long snouts)
1 and C

Words to know and Index

babies
pages 6–7

backbones
page 4

carnivores
pages 12–13, 18

crests
page 11

herbivores (plants)
pages 10–11, 16

frill

beak

horns
pages 16–17

plates (spines)
pages 14–15, 17, 22

reptiles
pages 4–5, 20–21

scales
page 5

Notes for adults

Objectives
- to help children learn about the features of reptiles that lived long ago
- to allow children to realize that they can read and remember even the most difficult words

Prerequisites
Ask the children to read *Reptile rap* before reading *What are dinosaurs?* By introducing children to dinosaurs via *Reptile rap*, some reptile features will be more familiar to them.

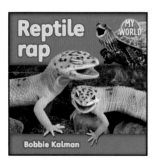

Guided Reading: F

Questions before reading *What are dinosaurs?*
"Which dinosaurs can you name?"
"Have you ever seen dinosaur bones in a museum?"
"Which long bone is in the back of a dinosaur that is also in your back?"
"Which reptiles today are most like dinosaurs?"
(The word "dinosaur" means "terrible lizard," but dinosaurs were not lizards. They were more like alligators and crocodiles.)

Class discussion
Read the book to the children. Pronounce the names of the dinosaurs and ask the children to say the names back to you. Write the names on a board or chart paper after you say them.
Then ask the children to look for clues that will help them remember each dinosaur, such as: walking on two or four legs; herbivore or carnivore; crests on head; plates and clubs on body; horns, frills, and beaks; biggest size. What did dinosaurs and the reptiles of today have in common? (scales, backbones, hatching from eggs) Why were the animals on pages 20-21 not dinosaurs?

Extension
How many children were able to identify the similar features of the dinosaurs and other animals shown on page 22? Did they match any animals based on other features, such as color or number of legs?

For teacher's guide, go to www.crabtreebooks.com/teachersguides

24